Yuri Life

No Love, No Life!

Kurukuruhime

CONTENTS

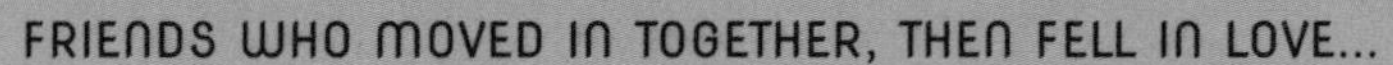

FRIENDS WHO MOVED IN TOGETHER, THEN FELL IN LOVE...

A Laid-Back Life Together

Room 1

Manami Hanazono (31)
Occupation: Web Designer
Likes games (and she's good). Likes quirky stuff.

Yuuna Miyafuji (27)
Occupation: Illustrator
Likes games (but she's lousy). Likes new things.

SOOOO (SNEAK)
KAKI (SKRIT)
かき
KAKI
かき
KAKI
かき
HYOKO (PEEK)
ひょこ
DWEH!?
WHAT ARE YOU WRITING?
Manami
Yuuna
WHAT THE—!?
ARE YOU IN GRADE SCHOOL!?
WE'RE...
...PAST THE SWEETHEART UMBRELLA STAGE, YOU KNOW.
SO LIKE THIS?
KYU (SQUEAK)
キュ
Manami
Yuuna
KYU
キュッ
NOW, THAT'S MORE LIKE IT!

I'M BEAT.
MAAANA-CHAAAN!
MAKE ME FEEL BETTER!
PIIII (SQUEEEAL)
SURE.
C'MON, GET OVER HERE.
BA (JUMP)
HUH? WHAT?
I, UM... I REEK OF HERBAL COMPRESSES RIGHT NOW.
I DON'T CARE.
C'MERE. C'MERE!
NYO (WILT)
NOOO...
IT'S ALL RIGHT.
THERE, THERE.
THERE'S NO ROMANCE IN THIS. I HATE THAAAT...
OH, BUT THERE'S LOVE.

WEEEEE AAARE AAALIEEENS...
HUH?
WOW, THAT TAKES ME BACK.

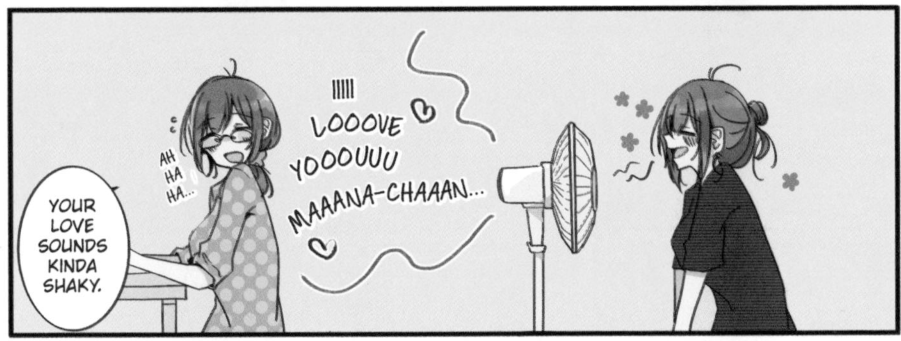
LOOOVE YOOOUUU MAAANA-CHAAAN...
AH HA HA...
YOUR LOVE SOUNDS KINDA SHAKY.

じっ...
JI (STARE)
HUH?

I LOVE YOU!
MY FEELINGS ARE ROCK-SOLID!!
AND I LOVE YOU TOO.

BAAAH...
MY EDITOR REJECTED MY IDEA AGAIN.
DARAAAA (LOLL)
WHAT DOES "REALITY" MEAN ANYWAY?
YOU WORKED HARD TODAY.
WANT A DRINK?
THANKS!
YES!
REAL ROMANCE...
...DOES IT REALLY NEED THAT MUCH THOUGHT?
I MEAN, JUST YOU BEING HERE MAKES ME HAPPY, MANA-CHAN.
I DON'T THINK I COULD BE HAPPIER.
IT'S INCREDIBLE.
THAT'S, UM...
THANK YOU?
CHEERS!
MM-HM!
THANK YOU TOO!

ぼろっ
BORO (RATTY)
YUMMY
しょぼー
SHOBOOO (BUMMED)
I THINK THIS IS ONE FOR THE RAG BAG.
HUH?
AWW!
I HAVE SOME GREAT MEMORIES WITH THAT SHIRT.
THERE, THERE.
WE'LL BE TOGETHER UNTIL THE NEXT ONE'S ALL SAGGY TOO.
OKAY?
!
WE'LL BE TOGETHER EVEN AFTER WE GET ALL SAGGY!
UH...
I'D REALLY RATHER NOT GET ALL SAGGY.
HA HA!
ぱん
PAN (FWAP)

DO THOSE ME●RHYTHM MASKS WORK?
YEAH... PRETTY WELL, I GUESS.
GOOD TO KNOW.
ちゅっ CHU (SMOOCH)
!
にへー NIHEEEE (GRIN)
...DID YOU JUST KISS ME?
WHY, YES, I DID.
AAAAAGH!
I WISH THIS WAS A ROMANTIC BLINDFOLD, NOT A ME●RHYTHM!
WHAT'S A ROMANTIC BLINDFOLD?
ばた BATA (KICK)
LIKE A LOVER'S STOCKINGS OR SOMETHING!
THAT... MIGHT BE MORE KINKY THAN ROMANTIC.
ばた BATA

THEY SAY "LOVE" ONLY LASTS THREE YEARS.
THAT'S A SHOCK.
HOW ABOUT THAT?

SINCE HIGH SCHOOL, SO...
UM... IT'LL BE TEN YEARS SOON.

...WHAT YEAR ARE WE ON?

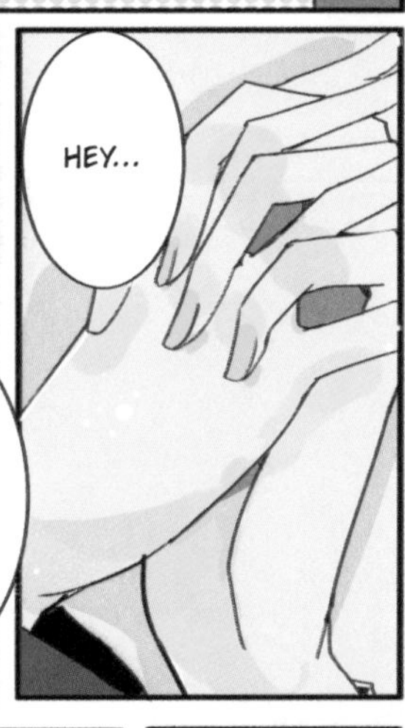

I LOVE YOU.
I LOVE YOU LOTS, FOREVER AND EVER.
MM-HMM!
RIGHT BACK AT YOU!

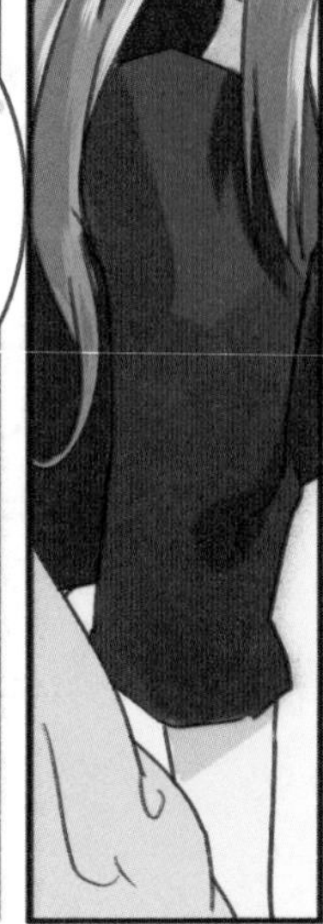

AND THEY LIVED HAPPILY EVER AFTER!

No Love, No Life!

IT'S IRRITATING, BUT SHE'S THE ONE I CAN REALLY BE MYSELF AROUND...

A Love-Hate Life Together

DROPPING DISHES... YOU'RE HOPELESS.
HA HA!
THAT HAPPENED 'COS YOU HUGGED ME, AYA.
THAT SHRIEK WAS SO CUTE...

I'M TOTALLY GOING TO FIND A BETTER DISH THAN YOU.
YEAH, YEAH.

WELL, LET'S PICK OUT NEW ONES AND MEET UP BACK HERE.

THIS IS CUTE!

THAT ONE'S NOT BAD.

......

WHY DID YOU PICK THE SAME ONE?
ARE YOU DUMB?
YOU'RE DUMB, AREN'T YOU?
...WANT TO GET THEM?
I SHOULD BE ASKING YOU THAT.

IT'S ALMOST ALWAYS MILD

SPICY!

MILD!

MOGYAAASU (SCREECH)

もぎゃーす

WE JUST HAD MILD, REMEMBER?

AND IT'S NOT LIKE YOU DON'T EAT SPICY FOOD.

BUT WITH THE MILD KIND, YOU CAN TELL HOW IT TASTES!!

I ALWAYS WANT IT MILD!

GUI (TUG)

OH, FOR CRYING OUT LOUD!

I JUST HAD SOMETHING SWEET, SO...
...LET'S GO WITH SPICY THIS TIME. ALL RIGHT?
OKAY......

I LOVE YOU.

HUNH? WHA—!?
GUNYO (SPLORT)
LOOK, IT'S FINE ONCE IN A WHILE, ISN'T IT?
JUST ONCE IN A WHILE...

CAN IT. NOT WHILE WE'RE BRUSHING OUR TEETH.
I MEAN, YOU'RE SUPER-CUTE, AND I CAN'T DO ANY-THING.
SHAKOOO (SHAKKA)
WHY NOT JUST USE YOUR WORDS?
......I LOVE YOU, MORON.

I'M DONE WITH MY BATH.
OH. OKAY.
BUOOOO (VROOOSH)
HEY!
YOU USED MY SHAMPOO.
SO WHAT? IT'S NO BIG DEAL.
I WAS OUT OF MINE.
YOU'RE OUT OF YOUR MIND, THAT'S WHAT.
IS TOO.
IT'S MORE EXCITING IF YOU DON'T SMELL ALIKE. THAT'S WHAT I READ THE OTHER DAY.
YOU DON'T HAVE TO WORRY ABOUT THAT. I'M LITERALLY ALWAYS EXCITED ANYWAY.
...WELL, I AM.
WAS THAT TOO CUTE?
SORRY.
LEAVE ME ALONE.
WHATEVER. IT'S FINE.

すぃよ
SUIYO
すぃよ
SUIYO (SNOOZE)
すよー
SUYOOO (ZZZ)
きゅん
KYUN (TWINGE)
Good morning.
ちゅっ
CHU (SMOOCH)
I'M GONNA MAKE TODAY ANOTHER GOOD OOOOONE!
WHY DID SHE KISS ME!?

I TOLD YOU YOU'D CATCH A COLD IF YOU DIDN'T BUNDLE UP WHEN YOU SLEPT.
WELL, YOU STOLE ALL THE BLANKETS...
YOU'RE ALL OVER THE PLACE WHEN YOU SLEEP.

ANY SPECIAL REQUESTS?
THAT YUMMY PUDDING YOU GOT THE OTHER DAY.
BUY ME SOMETHING TO DRINK TOO.
OKAY, OKAY.

YOU'D BE CUTE IF YOU WERE ALWAYS THIS UNCOMPLICATED.
HUNH!?
AREN'T I ALWAYS CUTE!?

WELL...
...YES, YOU'RE CUTE, BUT...

MAYBE YOU SHOULD CHECK YOUR OWN TEMPERATURE, AYA.
WHAT WAS THAT!?

AND THEY LIVED HAPPILY EVER AFTER!

HOW THE HELL CAN YOU EVEN SERVE CUSTOMERS WITH AN ATTITUDE LIKE THAT!? (LOL)

YEAH, WELL, YOU LOOK MORE LIKE A LOAN SHARK THAN A BANK TELLER!

WORK CLOTHES

No Love, No Life!

ハへ

A CHANCE ENCOUNTER WITH HER DREAM LOVER AT THE LIBRARY...
Life with a Writer
Room 3
Hotaru Mejiro (19) Occupation: Library Clerk
Conflicted about how to act around Kei since she's both her fan and her lover. Adores books.
Kei Tsubameno (28) Occupation: Writer
Met Hotaru at the library, fell in love at first sight, and brought her home. Wants to act cool since Hotaru is both her fan and her lover...but being crazy about Hotaru makes that impossible.

HRRRN... IT'S DONE...
I FINISHED, BUT I DUNNO ABOUT THIS.
YOU WROTE A NEW NOVEL? LET ME READ IT!
YOU BET.
I WANT YOU TO BE THE FIRST TO READ EVERYTHING I WRITE.

SO YOU SAID YOU DIDN'T KNOW ABOUT THIS...
YOU'RE NOT FEELING CONFIDENT ABOUT IT?
NO, THAT'S NOT IT.
IT'S ANOTHER GOOD ONE.

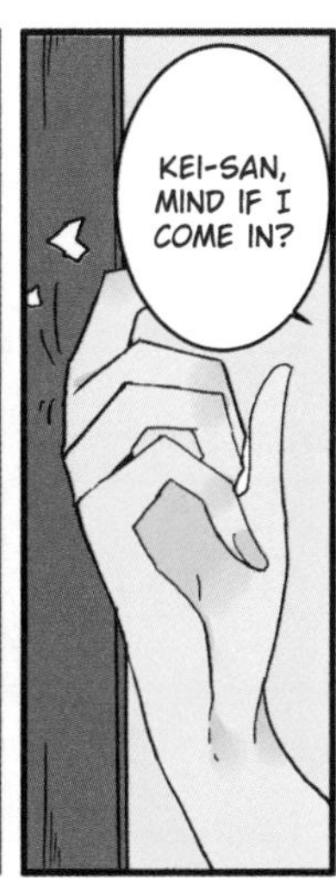
KEI-SAN, MIND IF I COME IN?

I MADE A MIDNIGHT SNACK. LET'S HAVE IT TOGETH...

SHE'S ASLEEP...

YOU KNOW...
...I'M CRAZY ABOUT YOU TOO.
どき DOKI
どき DOKI (BADUMP)
どき DOKI
どき DOKI
どき DOKI
SOME-THING SMELLS GOOD.
WHAT AN ADORABLE SNACK.

AAAUGH...
OH! UM!
I THOUGHT WE COULD HAVE A MIDNIGHT SNACK, SO...
MMM.
I COULD CERTAINLY GO FOR THE SNACK IN FRONT OF ME.
I LEFT IT OVER THERE!

SHEESH. SHE ALWAYS TEASES ME...
BATAN (SHUT)
ばたん
I LIKE KEI-SAN WHEN SHE'S HARD AT WORK ON A NOVEL...
...BUT IT DOES GET A LITTLE LONELY.
OH! IS THIS THE "HATING WHAT YOU FELL FOR" THING PEOPLE TALK ABOUT?
AGH!!
SOOOO (SNEAK)
MON (FRET)
MON
HMM...
BUT I DO LOVE KEI-SAN.
KEI-SAN!?
I'M SORRY FOR TEASING YOU WHEN YOU CAME IN TO SEE ME.
PLEASE DON'T HATE ME.
HONESTLY!
THIS ALWAYS HAPPENS, AND YOU KNOW IT.
DO YOU WANT THAT SNACK NOW?
YES. I THINK I'LL HAVE IT.

A BOOK SIGNING, HUH...?

BEFORE WE BECAME AN ITEM, I ALWAYS LOOKED FORWARD TO EVENTS WHERE I COULD MEET KEI-SAN.

I WUVVED DIS!

THANKS! ♥

ほわん HOWAN (HAZE)

ほわん HOWAN

BUT NOW...

I WANT TO KEEP ALL THE WON-DERFUL THINGS ABOUT HER FOR MYSELF.

もち MOCHI

もち MOCHI (JEALOUS)

URGH...

I WANT TO BE THE ONLY ONE WHO HOLDS HER HAND.

!

I MAY'VE BEEN BETTER AT WISHING FOR KEI-SAN'S HAPPINESS WHEN I WAS JUST A FAN.

は— HAAA (SIIIGH)

GOOD JOB AT THE BOOK SIGNING.
THANKS. I'M NOT SURE HOW WELL IT ACTUALLY WENT.
HA HA...

ぎゅ…
GYU (CLUTCH)
KEI-SAN, LISTEN...

I CAN'T...
...LIVE WITH YOU ANYMORE.

HUH ......!?
WAS IT SOMETHING I DID? WHAT? HUH...?
あわっ
AWA (PANIC)
あわ
AWA

I USED TO BE GLAD TO SEE YOU GETTING MORE FAMOUS...
...BUT NOW, WATCHING YOU GET FURTHER AND FURTHER AWAY MAKES ME LONELY.
I THINK IT WAS EASIER FOR ME TO WISH FOR YOUR HAPPINESS WHEN I WAS JUST YOUR FAN.
I'M NOT FIT TO BE YOUR LOVER.

DON'T BE SO MEAN, HOTARU.
I'VE CHANGED TOO.
I MEAN, I'M HEAD OVER HEELS FOR YOU.
JUST BEING WITH YOU MAKES ME HAPPY.
SO...
...THINK OF YOUR OWN HAPPINESS, HOTARU.
...IN THAT CASE...

AND THEY LIVED HAPPILY EVER AFTER!

No Love, No Life!

LOVE AT FIRST SIGHT WITH A GIRL AT DEATH'S DOOR!?
Life with a Grim Reaper
Room 4
Saki Shinibana (Age Unknown)
Occupation: Grim Reaper
Does her best to resolve lingering worldly attachments so people can die without regret. Has an expressionless face, but the skull on her head is honest. (As naked bone, it has nothing to hide.)
Yuzu Ishibashi (25)
Occupation: Systems Engineer
A working adult who's always so busy that she's nearly lost sight of the point of living. The 2-D world is one of her few comforts. Generally tends to be a starry-eyed romantic.

FINALLY. HOME SWEET HOME.
I THINK I'LL SKIP DINNER AGAIN TONIGHT.
I'M BEAT...
I'M TOTALLY IN LOVE!!
WELCOME BACK.
......
UM... I'M HOME?
BONES... BONES...
DOSA (WHUMP)
ドサッ
BASA (FLAP)
ばさ
CUUUUTE!
ばさ
BASA
WHO IS THIS!!?
I SHOULD INTRODUCE MYSELF.
HUP!
I'M SAKI SHINIBANA.
A GRIM REAPER.
CHARMED...
I CAME TO PICK YOU UP.
SAAAA (BLANCH)
A GRIM...
...REAPER...
HUH...?
SO I'M GONNA DIE?
DON'T DIIIE...
YES. QUITE SOON UNFORTU-NATELY.

I'LL BE HELPING YOU PASS ON WITHOUT REGRETS.

IS THERE ANYTHING YOU'D LIKE TO DO BEFORE YOU GO?

NOTHING IN PARTICULAR...

PLEASE DON'T KEEP TALKING ABOUT DEATH...

CAUSE OF DEATH: CARDIAC EPISODE?

PAY ATTENTION TO MEEE!
WHAT IS THAT? YOU DO IT CON-STANTLY.
IT'S A ROMANCE GAME.

THE HEROINE GETS KILLED BY HER LOVER, WHO'S GOTTEN CURSED AND GONE INSANE, AND THE LOVER FOLLOWS HER.
THEN THEY FALL INTO HELL AND SPEND ETERNITY TOGETHER.
...
SHE'S HAVING FUN. HOW CUTE!
BUN
ぶん
BUN (FLAIL)
ぶん

GETTING TO DIE WITH THE ONE YOU LOVE WOULD BE WONDERFUL, WOULDN'T IT?
LOVERS' SUICIDE MOE!
ふぅ
PHEW!
DO YOU THINK SO?

I'D WANT THE PERSON I LOVE TO LIVE.
THEN I'D STAY WITH THEM FOREVER.
I SAID IT BECAUSE I AM A GRIM REAPER.

GESHI (KICK)
げし
GESHI
げし
OWWW!
IS THAT ANYTHING FOR A GRIM REAPER TO SAY?

...SAKI?

"GRIM REAPER" MEANS...

GOOD WORK
おつ

TO YUZU

...A LETTER?

IT'S BLACK...

YAY.

I'M LONELY...

YOUR LIFE HAS BEEN EXTENDED, YUZU-SAN. I'M SO HAPPY FOR YOU. SINCE YOU DON'T NEED ANYONE TO COME FOR YOU ANYMORE, I'M GOING HOME. MAKE SURE TO KEEP EATING PROPERLY. —SAKI

AND HERE SHE SAID SHE'D MAKE ME FALL FOR HER BEFORE I DIED.

SAKI... WEREN'T YOU GOING TO GIVE ME A GRAND ROMANCE?

IT'S BEEN THREE MONTHS SINCE SAKI DISAPPEARED.

SASAKI-SAN, LET'S GO EAT.

I DON'T NEED DINNER TODAY.

I'VE STILL GOT WORK TO CATCH UP ON.

I'M STILL DOING VERY WELL.

NOT ALLOWED. I CAN'T HAVE YOU GETTING TAKEN AWAY BY A GRIM REAPER, SASAKI-SAN.

THAT JOKE AGAIN? YOU LIKE THAT ONE, DON'T YOU?

AH HA HA...

IT'S SUPER-CUTE.

I'LL LIVE A LONG LIFE, SAKI.

COME HOME ONCE IN A WHILE, WOULD YOU?

HUH? NAH, YOU SHOULD COME SPEND THE NIGHT WITH ME AT THE OFFICE, YUZU-CHAN.

WOULD YOU BELIEVE IT? I ENDED UP GOING OUT WITH SASAKI-SAN, AND MY WISH FOR A GRAND ROMANCE CAME TRUE.

NEXT TIME I SEE YOU, LET ME THANK YOU PROPERLY, OKAY?

SHE'S MIIIIINE...
I'LL BE WAITING FOR YOU IN HELL.

AND THEY LIVED HAPPILY EVER AFTER...?

?
...

No Love, No Life!

TEACHER AT SCHOOL, LOVER AT HOME
Life with Sensei
Room 5
Michiru Shirai
(27)
Occupation: Japanese Language Teacher (Year 2)
An adult who hasn't quite grown up yet. An oldest daughter who talks tough and is bad at being pampered. A lazy busybody.
Ichika Kurosawa
(16)
Occupation: High School Third-year
Somewhat antisocial, so doesn't fit in at school. Has the hots for her teacher.

SENSEI?
YES?
HELP ME WITH MY HOME-WORK?
SURE.
WHAT SUB-JECT?
AWW, COME ON!
WHEN YOUR ADORABLE STUDENT WANTS YOU TO TEACH HER...
...THE SUBJECT IS OBVIOUSLY PHYSICAL EDUCATION, DUH!
YOU DON'T GET HEALTH AND PHYS ED HOME-WORK.
GYUMUUU (SQUISH)
SENSEI, DIS ISH CORPORAL PUNIF-MENT.
I'M YOUR GIRL-FRIEND RIGHT NOW.
SO, WHAT, YOU DON'T WANNA MAKE OUT?
WELL, I'M A GROWN-UP, YOU KNOW.
BEING IN THE MOOD AND SUCH IS IMPORTANT TO ME.
BUT THE TRUTH IS, I ACTUALLY DO WANT TO.

AGH...

IT'S DELISH. REALLY.

にごぉ〜〜

NIGOOOOO (GRIMACE)

OH YEAH? COULD YOU EAT IT EVERY DAY?

IF IT MEANS I CAN BE WITH YOU, I'LL DO MY BEST.

...I'M SORRY.

SO THERE'RE THINGS YOU CAN'T DO, HUH, SENSEI?

THAT'S JUST THE WAY IT IS.

LIVING ALONE, IT'S FASTER TO BUY FOOD.

THIS'LL BE THE FIRST HOME-COOKED MEAL YOU'VE HAD IN AGES.

I BET IT'LL BE SO GOOD YOU'LL ASK ME TO MARRY YOU.

YEAH, RIGHT.

PLEASE BE MY WIFE.
YUM...
BUT OF COURSE!

Haaaaah...

I KNEW IT. NOW THAT WE BOTH LIVE HERE ...

...I CAN'T BE THE TEACHER SHE IDOLIZED.

MOVING IN TOGETHER WAS A BAD IDEA...

IT'S EXHAUST-ING...

SENSEI!
LET'S TAKE A BATH.

I DON'T WANT HER TO HATE ME...
YEAH, SURE. BE RIGHT THERE.

THE BATH AT YOUR PLACE IS HUUUUGE, SENSEI. IT'S GREAT.
IT'S PRETTY SMALL FOR TWO, THOUGH.

HM?

SENSEI! SPIDER!
HUH!?
WHERE!? WHERE!? WHEEERE !?

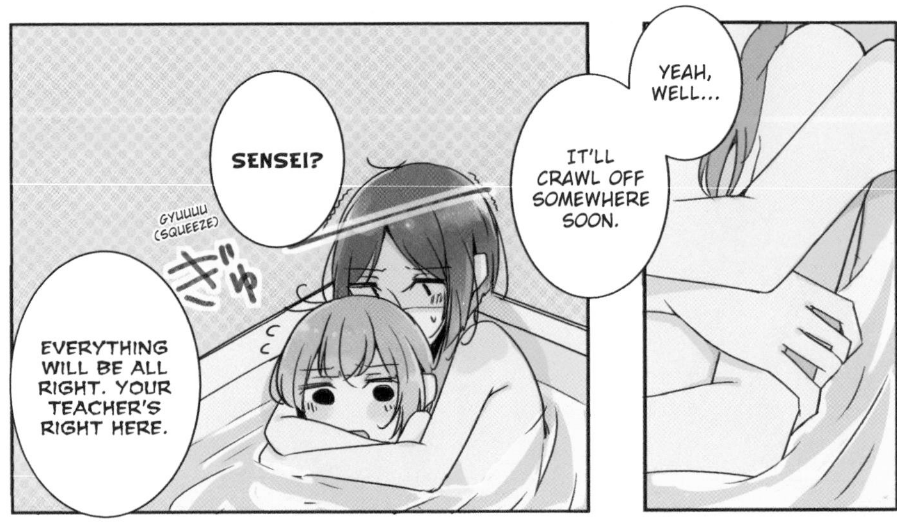
YEAH, WELL...
IT'LL CRAWL OFF SOMEWHERE SOON.
SENSEI?
ぎゅ
GYUUUU (SQUEEZE)
EVERYTHING WILL BE ALL RIGHT. YOUR TEACHER'S RIGHT HERE.

LIGHTS OUT.
'KAAAY.
MICCHAN?
ARE YOU PUSHING YOURSELF TOO HARD?
WHERE DID THAT COME FROM?
NO, I'M NOT.
"MICCHAN"...
REEEALLY?
GOOD QUES-TION.
ADULTS ARE LIARS, YOU KNOW.
SO YOU ARE OVERDOING IT.

IT'S GOTTEN PRETTY LATE.

SENSEI, I'M DONE!
THANKS.

......
YOU COULD'VE GONE HOME AHEAD OF ME, YOU KNOW.

WELL, SENSEI...
GETTING TO GO HOME WITH THE ONE YOU LOVE, TO THE HOUSE WHERE THEY LIVE...
DOESN'T THAT MAKE YOU INCREDIBLY HAPPY?

......
YOUNG PEOPLE ARE SO SIMPLE. MUST BE NICE.
WHAT ARE YOU TALKING ABOUT?
I MEAN, I FEEL A LITTLE BETTER NOW.

AND THEY LIVED HAPPILY EVER AFTER!

KASHA (CLICK)
カシャカシャカシャカシャ
KASHA
KASHA
KASHA

No Love, No Life!

現国
JAPANESE

SHE WANTS TO CAGE THE ONE SHE LOVES...
Life with a Yandere
Room 6
Runa Mitsudo (25)
Occupation: Beautician
Works independently. Wants Hina to stay at home all the time but thinks Hina will hate her if she says so. Has a collection she can't tell Hina about.
Hina Nidou (29)
Occupation: Trading Company Employee
Works for a major trading company. Flies all around the country because of her job, so she's rarely home for long.
YuRi

MOO...
I GOT AN AKABEKO BEFORE...
DID YOU? WELL, NOW IT HAS A FRIEND.
MATCHING GLASSES? BUT YOU'RE ALWAYS AWAY FOR WORK.
SORRY ABOUT THAT!
LET'S USE THEM TODAY!
...WHAT'S THIS?
I FOUND SOMETHING I THOUGHT WOULD LOOK GOOD ON YOU, SO I BOUGHT IT!
YOU REALLY DIDN'T NEED TO DO THAT.
YES, I DID!
THINK OF ME WHEN YOU WEAR IT, OKAY!?

AH HA HA...
THAT'S OKAY.
SORRY FOR ALWAYS GOING OFF ON BUSINESS TRIPS.
I'LL BUY YOU ANOTHER CUTE SOUVENIR NEXT TIME!

IT'S NOT THE GIFTS THAT ARE IMPORTANT. I'D BE HAPPY JUST HAVING HINA-CHAN HERE, BUT...

THANKS FOR ALWAYS CUTTING MY HAIR.
OH, IT'S NO TROUBLE.
ウき
UKI (HAPPY)
るん
RUN (BOUNCY)
YOUR HAIR FEELS NICE, AND IT SMELLS GOOD, SO CUTTING IT IS FUN.
OH, STOP WITH THE COMPLIMENTS.
YOU'RE EMBARRASSING ME.

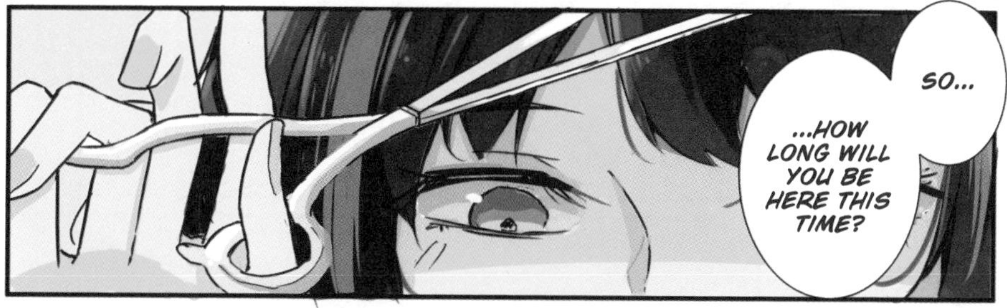
SO...
...HOW LONG WILL YOU BE HERE THIS TIME?

I MIGHT BE ABLE TO STAY FOR QUITE A WHILE.

THE NEXT BUSINESS TRIP IS OVERSEAS, SO THIS IS MY PRE-TRIP VACATION.
I CAN'T WAIT TO GO ABROAD.

I SEE.
I'LL LOOK FORWARD TO MY SOUVENIR, THEN.

THERE!
YOU'RE AS CUTE AS CAN BE NOW, HINA-CHAN!
OH, HONESTLY...
I TOLD YOU! THAT'S TOO MANY COMPLIMENTS!

AFTER I SWEEP UP YOUR HAIR, LET'S EAT.
WAIT JUST A MINUTE.
THANKS FOR DOING ALL THIS.
REALLY, IT'S FINE.

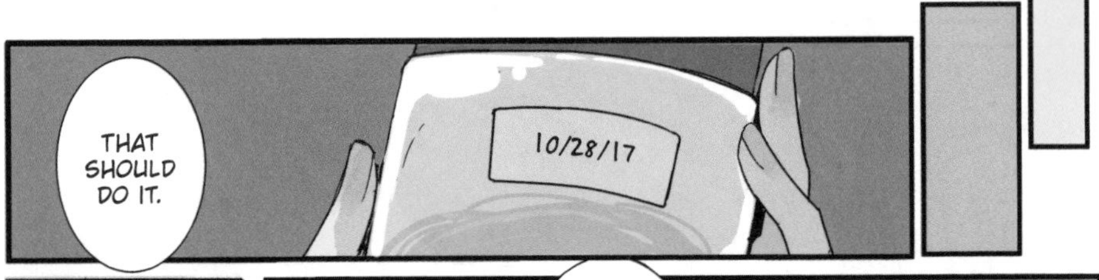
10/28/17
THAT SHOULD DO IT.

IF HINA-CHAN FOUND OUT I KEEP ALL HER CUT HAIR...
...I'M NOT SURE SHE'D EVER COME BACK HERE.

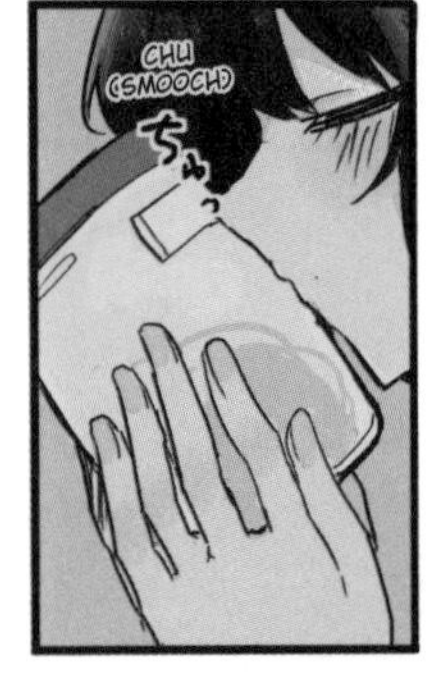
CHU (SMOOCH)

I WANT TO BE WITH HER ALL THE TIME.
IF ONLY I COULD JUST SHUT HER UP IN A JAR TOO...
RIGHT, HINA-CHAN?

A BUSINESS TRIP ABROAD, HM?
I EARN ENOUGH FOR BOTH OF US...
I WONDER IF RUNA WOULD COME WITH ME.
I'M LONELY!
ALL DONE!
WOW!
RUNA-CHAN, YOU REALLY ARE GOOD AT CUTTING HAIR.
......
I'LL BECOME A FANTASTIC BEAUTICIAN.
SO...
...LET ME BE THE ONLY ONE TO CUT YOUR HAIR, HINA-CHAN.
AND THEN...
...SHE WORKED REALLY HARD, AND SHE DID BECOME A BEAUTICIAN.
は――…
HAAAA (SIGH)
WOULD IT BE SELFISH TO ASK HER TO QUIT HER JOB AND COME WITH ME?
I'M NOT LIKE RUNA. SHE CAN DO ANYTHING.
ALL I CAN DO IS GIVE PEOPLE THINGS.
もふ
MOFU (MOOSH)
I'LL HAVE TO WORK HARDER AT MY JOB.

THE NIGHT BEFORE THE TRIP

RUNA, AREN'T YOU GOING TO SLEEP?
NOPE. I'LL STAY AWAKE TILL MORNING.
YOU LEAVE TOMORROW, DON'T YOU? I WANT TO LOOK AT YOU FOR AS LONG AS I CAN.
YOU'RE JOKING AGAIN...
YOU'LL SLEEP ONCE I'M ASLEEP, WON'T YOU?
OH, I DON'T KNOW ABOUT THAT.
YOU'LL FIND OUT ONCE YOU FALL ASLEEP, HINA-CHAN.
IF I'M ASLEEP, I WON'T KNOW!
HINA-CHAN'S GOING AWAY TOMORROW.
GO ON. YOU HAVE TO GET UP EARLY, DON'T YOU?
YOU'D BETTER GET TO SLEEP QUICK.

HINA-CHAN...
すよー
SUYOOOO (SNOOZE)
IF I BROKE THOSE PRETTY LEGS OF YOURS, WOULD IT STOP YOU LEAVING ME?
IF I SNIPPED OFF THOSE SMALL, SLIM FINGERS, WOULD I BE THE ONLY ONE YOU TOUCHED?
IF I GOUGED OUT YOUR JEWEL-LIKE EYES, WOULD YOU LOOK ONLY AT ME?
THERE'S NO WAY IT'S ALL RIGHT TO DO ANYTHING THAT AWFUL TO SOMEONE I LOVE, AND YET...
WHAT IS IT THAT MAKES ME WANT TO SHUT YOU UP INSIDE A JAR?
すよ すよ
SUYO SUYO
SHE'S SO CUTE...
I LIKE HER TOO MUCH. IT'S MADE ME A WEIRDO...
...EVEN THOUGH HINA-CHAN HASN'T CHANGED AT ALL.

AND THEY LIVED HAPPILY EVER AFTER...?

● The two of them during the business trip

IT'S BEEN THIRTY-SIX MINUTES SINCE I LAST MESSAGED HER, SO...
IT'S STILL TOO SOON...

WELL, SHE'S A BEAUTICIAN. I BET SHE'S BUSY.
HRRRM...

No Love, No Life!

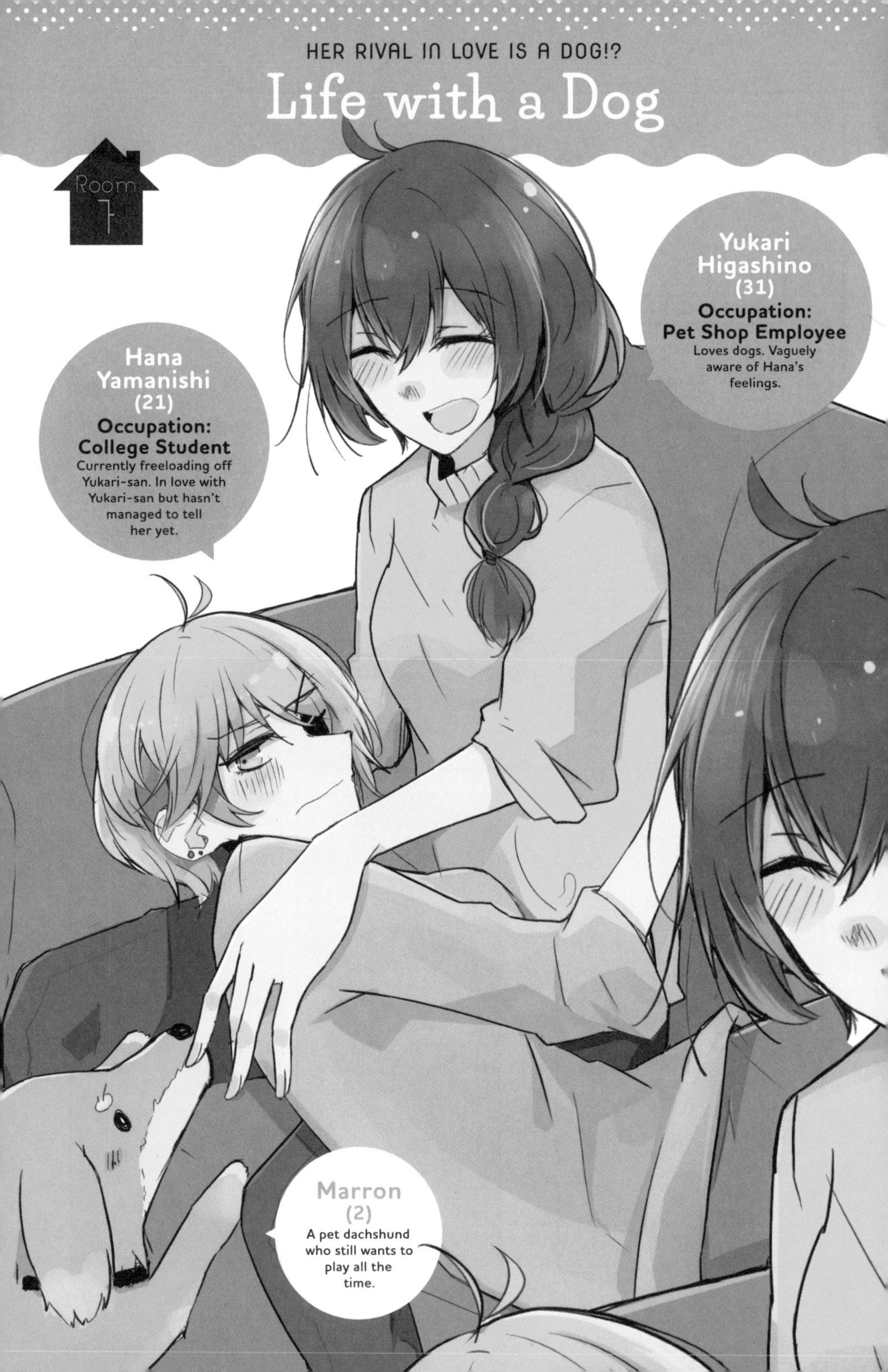
HER RIVAL IN LOVE IS A DOG!?
Life with a Dog
Room 7
Yukari Higashino
(31)
Occupation: Pet Shop Employee
Loves dogs. Vaguely aware of Hana's feelings.
Hana Yamanishi
(21)
Occupation: College Student
Currently freeloading off Yukari-san. In love with Yukari-san but hasn't managed to tell her yet.
Marron
(2)
A pet dachshund who still wants to play all the time.

I WISH YUKARI-SAN WOULD PAY ATTENTION TO ME TOO.
ARRRGH!
I WANNA BE A DOG!

NADE (PET)
NADE
WHAT A GOOD GIRL!
YES, YOU ARE! AREN'T YOU JUST THE CUTEST!?

GUI (TUG)

HUUUH!?
THERE, SEE? LOOK, HANA-CHAN, LOOK.

MARRON GOT JEALOUS.
WHAT ABOUT MEEEE!?

HOW ADOR-ABLE!

WHAT'S WRONG?
NOTHING.

THIS IS IT!
TODAY'S THE DAY I TELL HER I LIKE HER!
AREN'T YOU COMING TO BED?
NYU (POP)
I LO—
YUKARI-SAN!
~~~~!
MAYBE HE THOUGHT WE WERE PLAYING.
WHY DON'T WE ALL SLEEP TOGETHER TONIGHT?
LOVE RIVAL...
~~~~

IT'S TIME TO GET UP.

ゆすり
YUSURI (SHAKE)
ゆすり
YUSURI

NNNN... WHAT...?

THIS EARLY IN THE MORNING AND ALREADY YOU WANT CUDDLES!

HUH!?
UM...!
あわわわわ
AWA (PANIC)
WA WA WA
!

I'M SO SORRY. I THOUGHT YOU WERE MARRON.
わしゃ
WASHA (SKRITCH)
WASHA
WASHA
IT'S OKAY...
I, UM... I'M SORRY TOO...

I'M HOOOME.
YUKARI-SAN'S NOT OUT WALKING THE DOG TODAY.
PACHI (CLICK)
IS SHE SLEEPING?

YUKARI-SAN!?
...AND A NEW DOG!?

TO—
TOTEM POLE!
GASHIIII (LATCH)
UM...
WHAT ARE YOU TRYING TO DO?

U-UH...
UMM...
UMM...
WHAT SHOULD I DO AT A TIME LIKE—?

HERE.
THANK YOU.

THIS LITTLE ONE IS FROM THE SHOP.
SHE JUST WASN'T SELLING.
HUH...
DON'T PETS LIKE THAT GO TO THE POUND?
NO, NO. I WOULDN'T TAKE HER THERE.

SHE WAS ALL ALONE, AND NOBODY WANTED HER.

I FELT BAD FOR HER, SO...

...I WENT AND BROUGHT HER HOME WITH ME...

...EVEN THOUGH I'VE GOT MY HANDS FULL WITH THIS ONE ALREADY.

WELL, I'M HERE, AREN'T I!?

DOGS LIVE A PRETTY LONG TIME, YOU KNOW.
YOU'RE AT A FOUR-YEAR COLLEGE, AREN'T YOU?
UMM...
AFTER THAT...
IT'S FINE.
TEN YEARS FROM NOW...
...OR EVEN TWENTY...
...I'LL BE HERE WITH YOU, YUKARI-SAN.
YOU REALLY...
...DON'T MIND?

HMM...
...I'M NOT SURE MY FEELINGS GOT THROUGH TO HER.
WE DECIDED TO ADOPT THE DOG, BUT...
YOU TOO, YUKARI-SAN!?
WHY!?
THINGS LIKE THAT HAPPEN WHEN THERE ARE TWO.
WHA—!?
HEY!
MARRON!?
GUI (TUG)
HUH ...!?
WHAT!?
WHAT IS THIS!?
THERE WAS SOMETHING I WANTED TO CHECK.
WHAT YOU SAID BEFORE ...
CAN I ASSUME WE'RE IN...
...THIS SORT OF RELATION-SHIP NOW?

CALM DOWN!
YUKARI-SAN, WAIT, PLEASE.
WHAT'S GOTTEN INTO YOU ALL OF A SUDDEN?
SHE MADE HER CRY?
LOOK, THE DOGS ARE WATCHING US.
THE THING IS...
...I'VE LIKED YOU FOR AGES, HANA-CHAN.
YOU LIKE ME TOO, DON'T YOU?
YUKA—
WHAT I SAID ABOUT THE DOG... IT ISN'T TRUE.
I THOUGHT IF I MADE UP A SOB STORY ABOUT HER, YOU MIGHT STAY WITH ME.
HUH!?
I NEVER IMAGINED I'D FALL SO DESPERATELY IN LOVE AT MY AGE!
SINCE I LOVE YOU SO MUCH...
...I WON'T BE ABLE TO HOLD BACK IF WE KEEP LIVING TOGETHER, SO I'LL ASK YOU NOW.
IS YOUR LOVE THE KIND WHERE THIS ISN'T OKAY?
URK!

I DO LOVE HOW YUKARI-SAN TREASURES DOGS, THOUGH

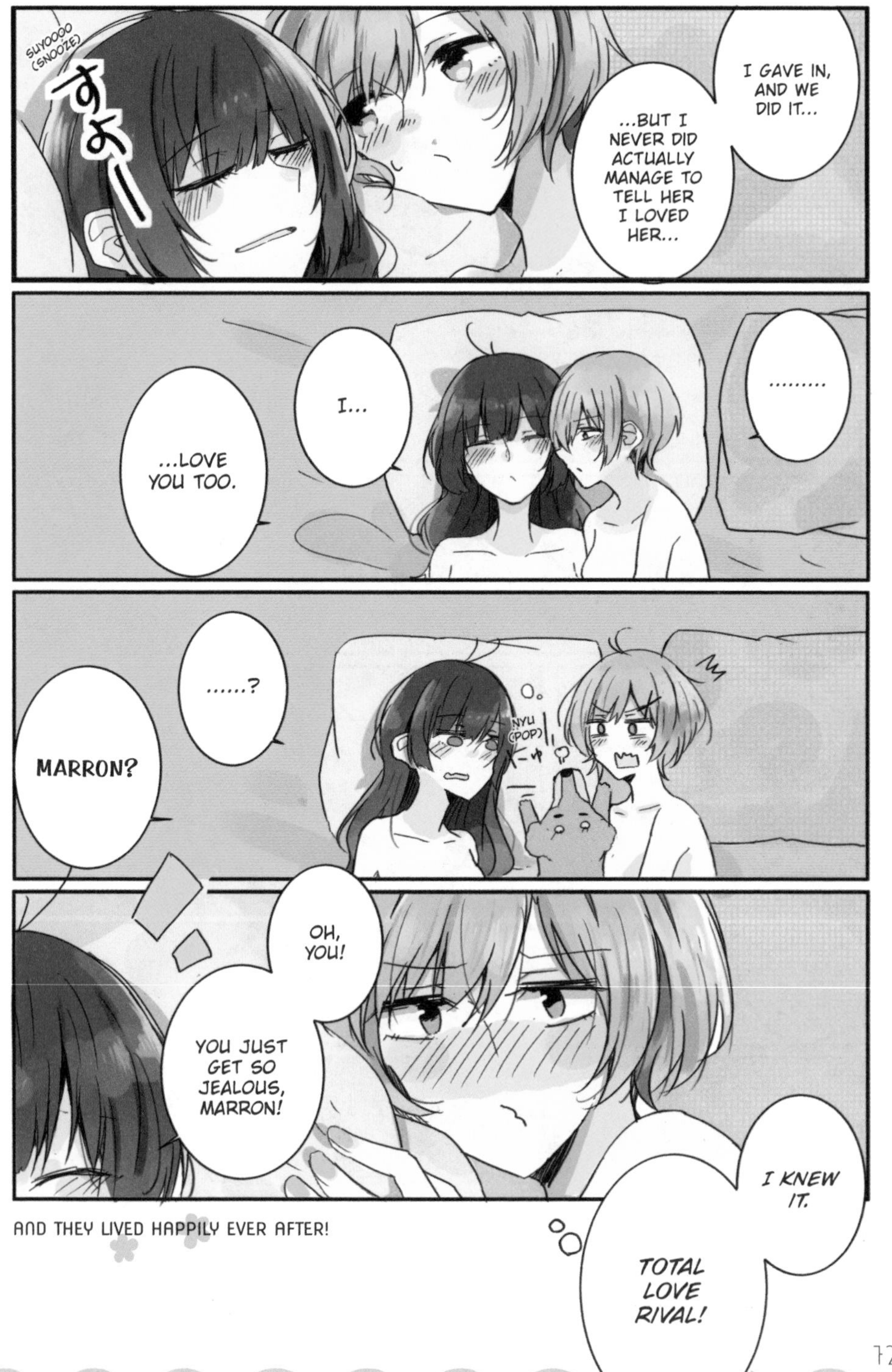

AND THEY LIVED HAPPILY EVER AFTER!

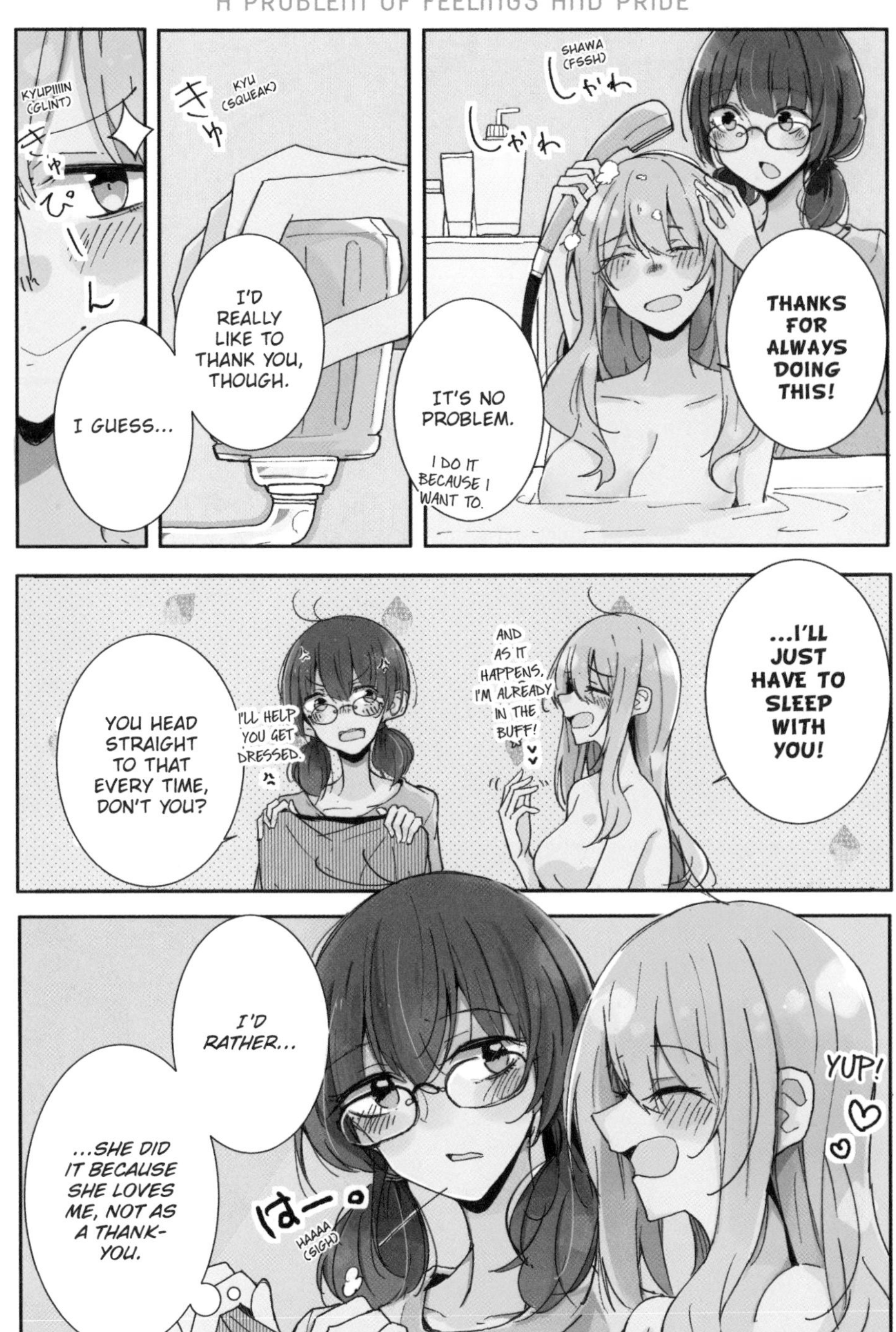
SHAWA (FSSH)
しゃわ しゃわ
THANKS FOR ALWAYS DOING THIS!
IT'S NO PROBLEM.
I DO IT BECAUSE I WANT TO.
KYU (SQUEAK)
きゅ
I'D REALLY LIKE TO THANK YOU, THOUGH.
KYUPIIIIN (GLINT)
きゅぴーん
I GUESS...
...I'LL JUST HAVE TO SLEEP WITH YOU!
AND AS IT HAPPENS, I'M ALREADY IN THE BUFF!
I'LL HELP YOU GET DRESSED.
YOU HEAD STRAIGHT TO THAT EVERY TIME, DON'T YOU?
YUP!
I'D RATHER...
...SHE DID IT BECAUSE SHE LOVES ME, NOT AS A THANK-YOU.
はー。
HAAAA (SIGH)

TWO PEOPLE FROM COMPLETELY DIFFERENT WORLDS UNDER ONE ROOF!?

Life with Little Miss Vixen

No Love, No Life!

LOOK...
...YOU COULD AT LEAST STICK AROUND UNTIL I'M DONE AT THE REGISTER.
TALK ABOUT A FREE SPIRIT...
LISTEN, I HEARD THIS FLOWER IS A TUBEROSE...
...AND ITS MEANING IS "DANGEROUS PLEASURES"!
YOU'RE HITTING ON ME!
I'M NOT HITTING ON YOU.
LET'S HURRY HOME BEFORE IT STARTS RAINING HARDER.

OH! THERE'S ONLY ONE UMBRELLA, SO...
YAAAY!
SWEET-HEART UMBRELLA!
POMU (BOMF)
ぽふっ
GUESS WHAT? THEY SAY THAT WITH SWEETHEART UMBRELLAS, THE ONE IN LOVE GETS WETTER.
PERVS!
WHAT GOES ON IN THAT HEAD OF YOURS?
HOW CAN YOU SAY ALL THIS RISQUÉ STUFF LIKE IT'S NOTHING?

YOU KNOW...
THAT WASN'T ACTUALLY RISQUÉ, WAS IT?

HUH?
THEN WHAT WAS IT?
GOOD QUESTION.

OH!
IF IT ISN'T MARI-CHAN!
WOW, IT'S BEEN AGES.
YOO-HOO! ♥
UMM... WHAT WAS YOUR NAME AGAIN?
IT WAS SOMETHING SHINY...
IT'S KIRARI.
...WHO'S THIS?
AN EX-GIRLFRIEND. ♥
...WHOSE NAME YOU DON'T REMEMBER. YOU SURE HAVEN'T CHANGED.
IS THIS YOUR LATEST GIRLFRIEND? SHE'S NOT YOUR USUAL TYPE.
HER LATEST...
PLAIN-LOOKING GIRLS LIKE HER ARE CUTE, AREN'T THEY?
KINDA LEWD!
OH, BUT IF YOU'RE GOING OUT WITH MARI-CHAN...
...MAYBE YOU'RE MORE INTO SEX THAN YOU LOOK?
HEE HEE!
HUH ...?
NO.
WE DON'T DO ANYTHING LIKE THAT... AT ALL.

OH. HUH.
SERIOUSLY!? SO, WHAT, YOU'RE JUST FRIENDS?
THAT'S NOT LIKE YOU, MARI-CHAN.
PERFECT TIMING, THEN.
GRR...
I'M NOT SEEING ANYONE RIGHT NOW.
WANT TO COME BACK TO MY PLACE, MARI-CHAN?
HMM? OH, GEE, I DON'T KNOW...
NAAADE (STROKE)
なーで
NAAADE
なーで
IT'S NOT AS IF I DON'T LIKE YOU, KIRARI-CHAN, BUT...
EXCUSE ME.
WOULD YOU PLEASE NOT HIT ON OTHER PEOPLE'S GIRLFRIENDS?
GUI (TUG)
ぐいっ
SHE'S MINE.

MASAKO-CHAN...
WE'RE GOING HOME.
HMM...
SO YOU WERE JUST EMBARRASSED BEFORE...
...AND YOU REALLY DO LOVE SEX?
IF THAT'S HOW IT IS, THEN...
...I'D BE FINE WITH ALL OF US GOING OUT TOGETHER.
YOU HEARD HER!
THREESOME, THREESOME!
WHAT I LIKE ISN'T SEX.
IT'S MARIN!
AND DON'T YOU ENCOURAGE HER!

START BY REMEMBERING NAMES

SO, MASAKO-CHAN...
...YOU LIKE ME, HUH?
WHA—!?

AND ALSO MAYBE SO YOU COULD MAKE FUN OF ME 'COS I CAN'T DO ANYTHING?
WHAT SORT OF PEOPLE HAVE YOU BEEN GETTING INVOLVED WITH?
AT LEAST LEARN TO TELL THE JERKS FROM DECENT TYPES.
UM...
WHY ELSE DID YOU THINK I WAS TAKING CARE OF YOU?
'COS YOU WANTED TO DO ME!

WHEN I'M WITH YOU, MASAKO-CHAN...
...I START THINKING, "I WONDER IF THIS IS WHAT THEY MEAN BY 'LOVE.'"
I'M A LITTLE JEALOUS OF THAT SIDE OF YOU.

I KNOW!
I'LL TRY HARD NOT TO FORGET YOUR NAME, MASAKO-CHAN.
EVEN THOUGH YOU FORGOT AN UNUSUAL NAME LIKE KIRARI?
WELL, GIVE IT YOUR BEST.

MASAKO-OOOOO.
MASAKO.
I HOPE I CAN MAKE MARIN HAPPIER THAN ANY OF HER EXES DID.

HEY!
WELCOME HOME!
WHAT ARE YOU DOING?
NAKED APRON.
YOU LIKE?
NOT THAT.
THE OTHER THING...
OH, THIS?
KIRARI-CHAN TAUGHT ME HOW TO MAKE IT.
IT'S CURRY.
SHOW ME HOW IT'S MADE.
YOU'RE GOING TO COOK, MARIN-CHAN?
I'M SURPRISED SHE ACTUALLY TAUGHT YOU.
AFTER ALL THAT...
I JUST HAVE TO PUT THE ROUX IN.
HANG ON A SEC.
POKI (SNAP)
ぽきっ
OH!
WHEN YOU PUT THE ROUX IN, YOU TURN OFF THE HEAT...
IS THAT RIGHT?
OF COURSE YOU'D KNOW.

!
WHAT'S THE MATTER?
N-NOTHING! NEVER MIND...
I FORGOT SHE WAS IN THAT STUPID GETUP!
I WAS TOO BUSY BEING SURPRISED SHE WAS COOKING.
SO WHAT SHOULD I DO NEXT?
FIRST PUT ON SOME CLOTHES!
TURN OFF HEAT, ADD ROUX, PUT ON CLOTHES. OKAY.
I'M WRITING IT ALL DOWN...
NEXT TIME, DON'T UNDRESS TO BEGIN WITH!

A STEP FORWARD?

MASAKO-CHAN.
THESE ARE FOR YOU!
SHE MADE A MESS AGAIN...
HUH!?
WHAT BROUGHT THIS ON?
FLOWERS ...?

I WANT TO THANK YOU, BUT...
...YOU KEEP TURNING DOWN SEX, SO...
I THOUGHT THESE MIGHT DO.
HMM...
YES, THESE FIT THE BILL FOR A THANK-YOU...

OHHHH! I'M GLAD YOU LIKE THEM!
PLEASE KEEP LOOKING OUT FOR ME, OKAY? ♥
DID SHE...
...PICK THESE OUT BECAUSE SHE WANTED TO MAKE ME HAPPY?
WELL, I GUESS THAT'S PROGRESS.

AND THEY LIVED HAPPILY EVER AFTER!

No Love, No Life!

H
(SEX)
No
H
(SEX)

NEW! THE YURI COHABITATION PROJECT LAUNCHES!
A Stage-Managed Life Together
Room 9
Fumi Kawase (28)
Occupation: Real Estate Site PR Officer
Young for her age. Tends to be physically affectionate. It seems there's someone she likes...
Minato Tooyama (25)
Occupation: Real Estate Site PR Officer
Likes sex but doesn't talk about it. Not good with physical affection. Has a one-sided crush on Fumi.

YURI CO-HABITATION PROJECT?

THAT'S RIGHT. WE'D LIKE THE TWO OF YOU TO LIVE IN AN APARTMENT WITH A MONTH-TO-MONTH LEASE...
...THEN POST HOW THINGS ARE GOING ON SOCIAL MEDIA.
すーっ
SUIIII (SCOOT)
UMM...
WHY US?

HA HA HA!

BECAUSE IT'S A REAL ESTATE PR PROJECT. THAT PUTS IT IN YOUR TERRITORY.

YES, BUT... WHY "YURI COHABITATION"?

WELL, MATURE LESBIANS ARE IN RIGHT NOW.

WE'VE GOT TO RIDE THE WAVE.

THAT'S PRETTY SIMPLISTIC THINKING...

Cohabitation Plan

OKAY, THEN!

THANKS FOR YOUR HELP ON THIS.

...YES'M.

I'VE DREAMED ABOUT THINGS LIKE WAKING UP TOGETHER

C-C-C-C-C-COHABITATION!?
"COHABITATION," SHE SAYS!
WHAT SORT OF THINGS ARE THEY HAVING US DO?
THE THING IS, I LIKE KAWASE-SENPAI.
I'VE FANTASIZED ABOUT LIVING WITH HER LIKE YOU WOULDN'T BELIEVE.
BUT NOT FOR A JOB LIKE THIS...
IT SAYS WE'LL BE COOKING TOGETHER.
I COULD HANDLE THAT...
AND THEY'VE ONLY GIVEN US ONE BED.
AH-HA-HA!
HUH...?
"PLEASE TAKE BATHS TOGETHER!" IT SAYS.
ぱああああ——
PAAAAAAAA (BEAM)
I'M LOOKING FORWARD TO THIS! HOW ABOUT YOU?
IT'LL BE LIKE A SLEEPOVER!
I CAN'T BE GENUINELY THRILLED ABOUT THIIIS!
I MEAN, I'M HAPPY, BUT...!!

DAY ONE: "COOKING TOGETHER"

SOWA そわ SOWA (FIDGET) そわ
WELL...
...IT'S FOR WORK. THERE'S NO GETTING OUT OF IT.
SOWA どき SOWA どき
OW!
WHAT'S WRONG?
I CUT MY FINGER.
THAT'S AWFUL.
PAKU (NOM) ぱくっ♡
AWE HOU OHAY?
KIDDING!
GASHAAAAN (CRASH) がしゃーん
AAAAAH!
THE CHOPPED VEGETABLES ...!

Kawase & Tooyama
On the first day, when I got nervous and cut my finger, Kawase-chan kissed it for me!
Even when we're in here cooking together, the kitchen's nice and roomy. (*´ω`*)

NOT JUST AS A PROJECT

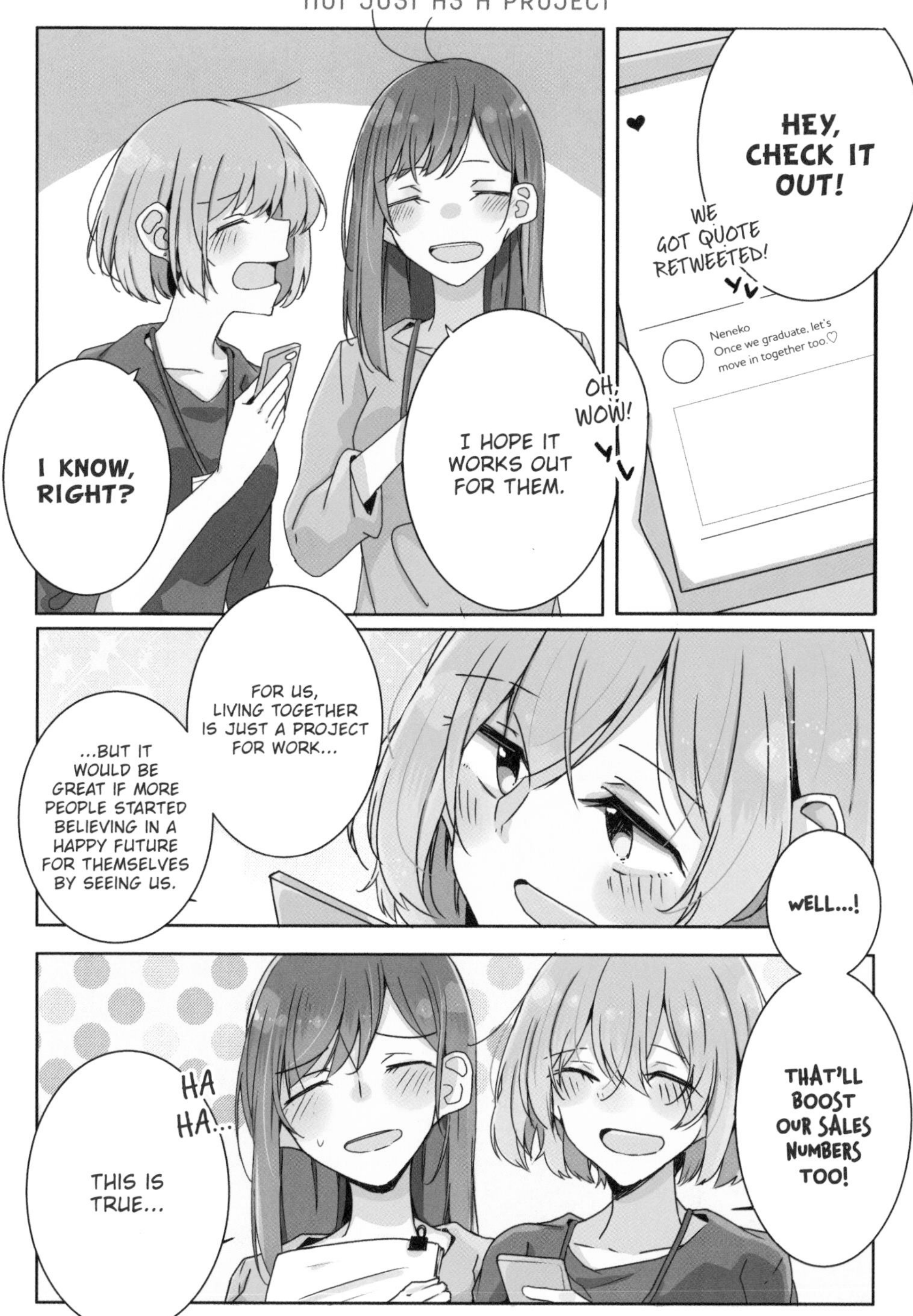

HEY, CHECK IT OUT!
WE GOT QUOTE RETWEETED!
Neneko
Once we graduate, let's move in together too.♡
OH, WOW!
I HOPE IT WORKS OUT FOR THEM.
I KNOW, RIGHT?
FOR US, LIVING TOGETHER IS JUST A PROJECT FOR WORK...
...BUT IT WOULD BE GREAT IF MORE PEOPLE STARTED BELIEVING IN A HAPPY FUTURE FOR THEMSELVES BY SEEING US.
WELL...!
THAT'LL BOOST OUR SALES NUMBERS TOO!
HA HA...
THIS IS TRUE...

THE PROJECT'S OFF!?
Kawase & Tooyama
5,421 Followers
Tweets & replies Media
WHY!? JUST LOOK HOW POPULAR IT IS!
LOOK AT ALL OUR FOLLOWERS!
THE POPULARITY IS ACTUALLY THE PROBLEM.
PEOPLE ARE SAYING, "DON'T MAKE A GAME OUT OF LESBIAN LOVE!"
WE AREN'T DOING THIS FOR FUN...
NOPE. IT'S FOR WORK.
BESIDES, YOU TWO WEREN'T ALL THAT INTO THE IDEA IN THE FIRST PLACE.
IT WAS JUST FOR WORK ANYWAY.
WELL, UM...
I'M PRETTY SURE KAWASE-SENPAI ALREADY LIKES SOMEONE, BUT...
IT... WASN'T.
NOT FOR ME.

SORRY.
I DIDN'T MEAN TO STARTLE YOU.
YES, WE'RE KILLING THE YURI COHABITATION PROJECT...
I WAS LIVING WITH YOU 'COS I WANTED TO.
TO BE HONEST, I'D ALREADY FANTASIZED ABOUT IT A TON.
...BUT IF I'D TOLD YOU SO, YOU WOULD'VE HAD TO QUIT EITHER WAY, WOULDN'T YOU?
IT WOULD JUST BE AWKWARD.
I GOT CARRIED AWAY AND HAD FUN WITH IT. I BET THAT CREEPED YOU OUT.
I'D THOUGHT IT WAS AN IMPOSSIBLE DREAM, SO EVEN IF IT WAS FOR WORK, I WAS HAPPY.
...IT WASN'T WHAT I WANTED.
YEAH, I FIGURED.
I'M SORRY.
THAT'S NOT WHAT I MEANT.

I DID WANT TO

KAWASE-SENPAI, WOULD YOU MOVE IN WITH ME?
NOT FOR WORK. ON A, UM, PERSONAL BASIS.
...I'LL TAKE BATHS WITH YOU THIS TIME, YOU KNOW?
UM, IF YOU WANT TO.
AND WE'LL SLEEP IN THE SAME BED.
...YES, IF YOU'RE OKAY WITH THAT.
ABSOLUTELY.
THERE WAS A LOT WE COULDN'T DO WHEN WE WERE LIVING TOGETHER FOR WORK, AFTER ALL.
NO, UM, SINCE IT WAS FOR WORK, I FELT BAD...
OH, HONESTLY!
FROM NOW ON, WE'RE GONNA DO ALL SORTS OF STUFF...
...WE COULDN'T DO DURING THE JOB, ALL RIGHT?

I HEAR THEY'RE GONNA START ACTIVELY SELLING...
...TO SAME-SEX COUPLES IN ORDER TO REACH THE CUSTOMERS THAT PROJECT ATTRACTED.
OOOOH!
WE WORKED HARD, SO...
...THE SALES DEPARTMENT HAD BETTER WORK JUST AS HARD.
AND WE'RE THE PR!
AIN'T THAT THE TRUTH!
MM. THIS IS NICE.
OOF.
HM? WHAT IS?
I JUST THOUGHT, "LIVING TOGETHER'S THE BEST!"
IT REALLY IS!

AND THEY LIVED HAPPILY EVER AFTER!

No Love, No Life!

WHEN I SAID I LIKED HER, SHE GOT ALL LOVEY-DOVEY...♡

A Steamrolled Life Together

SO...
IF WE HAVE TO...
...LET'S WRITE ON EACH OTHER'S OMELETS, MMKAY?
YEAH, YEAH.
DONE YET?
ALMOST.
THERE!
LOVE
LOVE"
"LOVE-LOVE"! THAT'S US!
GYUUU (SQUEEZE)
ぎゅ
......I GUESS SO.

OH!
ポロッ
PORO (SLIP)
SOMETHING FELL.

ME TOO.
I FELL.
IN LOVE!
TETEEEEN (TA-DAA)
てて～ん!!
YEAH, YEAH.

I ALSO...
DID YOU FALL?
DID YOU?
ARGH...
...YES.

CHANGE OF RESIDENCE FORM
ONCE I SEND THIS IN...
...I'LL FINALLY BE LIVING WITH MARI-CHAN OFFICIALLY.
THAT'S PRETTY INCREDIBLE.
ARE WE LOVERS?
I WONDER WHAT OUR RELATIONSHIP ACTUALLY IS.
"COHABITING"...
ぽち
POCHI (TAP)
ぽち
POCHI
...AND "RELATIONSHIP"...
Cohabiting, relationship
Fiancée or common-law wife
KYAAAA (SQUEAL)
キャー
WIFE!
I'M BACK!

WELCOME HOME...
...HONEY!
WHAT'S WITH YOU ALL OF A SUDDEN?
TERE (BLUSH)
てれ
TERE
てれ
RESIDENT CARD
IT'S JUST A PIECE OF PAPER...
...BUT IT MADE ME KINDA HAPPY.

NOT REALLY THAT DIFFERENT

THERE'S SOMETHING THAT'S BEEN WORRYING ME SINCE WE MOVED IN TOGETHER.

OH. DOING LAUNDRY?

I'LL HELP!

OVER HERE! PICK ME!

HOW AM I SUPPOSED TO INITIATE SEX?

BEFORE, WE JUST SORTA MADE SURE TO DO IT WHENEVER WE MET UP.

MON (FRET)

NOW THAT WE BOTH LIVE HERE, WE'RE ALWAYS TOGETHER, AND I'M NOT SURE WHEN IT'S OKAY.

MON

MON

MON

BUT YUNO REALLY IS CUTE, AND SO...UM...TO BE HONEST...

...I WANNA DO IT ALL THE TIME!

MARI-CHAN?

WHAT'S GOING THROUGH YOUR HEAD WHILE YOU'RE CLUTCHING MY PANTIES?

PERV!

OH, YOU!

N-NO, UM...!

YUNO, THERE'S AN OUTFIT I'D LIKE YOU TO TRY ON.
HM? WHAT IS IT?
THIS.
BUT THAT'S...
A WEDDING DRESS!?
UM...
IF YOU DON'T MIND, WOULD YOU PUT IT ON FOR ME?
I'M SO HAPPY!
I LOVE YOU, MARI-CHAN!
がばっ
GABA! (GLOMP)
YUNO!?
YOU'LL DRESS ME, WON'T YOU, MARI-CHAN?
SO LET ME UNDRESS YOU!
OKAY.
SURE.

AND THEY LIVED HAPPILY EVER AFTER!

No Love, No Life!

Special Room
A Laid-Back Couple
This is a carefully retouched reprinting of the A Laid-Back Couple web manga, which is where Laid-Back Life Together—the series before Yuri Life—began!

NO, NO. NOT AT ALL.
THANKS FOR THE FOOD.
IT'S FINE. I'LL TAKE CARE OF IT REAL QUICK.
OH, DON'T WORRY ABOUT THAT. I'LL CLEAN UP.
THANK YOU.
LOVE YOU.
YOU'RE EASY.
MM. MY DAY WAS PRETTY CHILL.
TO LOOK AT US NOW, YOU'D NEVER BELIEVE WHAT IT WAS LIKE WHEN WE WERE JUST STARTING OUT, WOULD YOU?

NEITHER OF US WAS USED TO LIVING TOGETHER OR TO OUR JOBS.
WE'D GET HOME FROM WORK, RUN OUT OF ENERGY, AND JUST CRASH.
SHE'S DEAD...
I DIDN'T MANAGE TO MAKE DINNER. SORRY...
OH, YEAH. THERE WAS THAT.
OR WE'D LEAVE EVERYTHING TO EACH OTHER, LEADING TO COLLAPSE.
IF YOU CAN'T...
...THEN JUST SAY SO.
OKAY...
WELL, BACK THEN...
...WE WERE DESPERATE TO BE LIKED.
'KAYYY! ALL DONE!
THANKS.
GREAT!
IN THAT CASE, HERE'S YOUR "GOOD JOB" POPSICLE!

YOU AREN'T DESPERATE NOW?
MM...
...WELL, I TRUST YOU TO KEEP LIKING ME, SO...
OOOH.
ぽろっ
PORO (DROP)
COLD!
OOPS...
......SORRY.
WHAT ELSE DID YOU EXPECT, EATING IT IN A PLACE LIKE THAT!?
I-I'LL GO GRAB YOU A TOWEL.

YOU'RE IN A GOOD MOOD.
BRRR!
BRR!
EH HEH HEH!
I GOT A NEW CELL PHONE.
OH?
IT DOESN'T LOOK THAT DIFFERENT.
IT IS, THOUGH. IT HAS FINGERPRINT AUTHENTICATION AND STUFF.
BY THE WAY...
ISN'T THAT A LITTLE FRUMPY?
...WHAT'S WITH THE OUTFIT? ARE YOU GOING OUT?
YOU'RE REALLY TOUGH, AREN'T YOU...
NO, I'M COLD.

I DID FEEL LIKE IT'D FINALLY STARTED TO COOL OFF A LITTLE.
SAY "CHEESE"!
ぱしゃ
PASHARIIII (KACHIK)
WHY DID YOU TAKE THAT?
'COS YOU'RE CUTE?
OOOH!
TALK ABOUT GORGEOUS!
WHAT? LET ME SEE.
GET A LOAD OF THE QUALITY ON THIS IMAGE! GORGEOUS, RIGHT?
EXCUSE YOU.
SO ONLY THE IMAGE QUALITY IS GORGEOUS?
THE SUBJECT IS GORGEOUS TOO, OF COURSE.
THAT'S BETTER.

....
WHY ARE YOU STRIPPING ME?
I'M CURIOUS ABOUT WHAT'S UNDER HERE.
I'M NOT SO SURE ABOUT THAT.
IT'S NORMAL TODAY.
JIIII (ZZZZZIP)
I WISH SHE'D JUST DO IT ALL AT ONCE...
KUWAAAA (GRAAWK)
DWAH!?

WHAT IS WITH THE FREAKY BIRD?
IT'S A POTOO. ISN'T IT CUTE?
NO. DEFINITELY NOT CUTE.
YOU HAVE WEIRD TASTE.
IT'S SCARY.
HUH?
AWW, BUT IT'S ADORABLE.
HERE WE GO.
ぱしゃー
PASHAAA (SNAP)
CAN I TWEET THAT MY WIFE WAS WEARING A WEIRD SHIRT?
SURE, I GUESS...
SHE MAY BE ON A CAMERA SPREE FOR A WHILE NOW...

IT'S BEEN A LONG TIME SINCE WE ATE OUT.
TOTALLY.
DOESN'T IT REMIND YOU OF WHEN WE'D JUST STARTED SEEING EACH OTHER?
IT'S A DATE.
WANT TO HOLD HANDS?
SHALL WE?
YAY!

....
NIGI (SQUEEZE)
にぎ
NIGI
にぎ
....
SURI (STROKE)
すり
SURI
すり
....
YOU KNOW...
I THINK THIS ACTUALLY GIVES ME MORE BUTTERFLIES NOW THAN IT USED TO...
YEAH...

WHAT KIND OF ROLLED OMELET DO YOU WANT? SWEET OR IN BROTH?
SWEET!
SARA (SIFT)
SARA
OKAY. SWEET OMELET COMING RIGHT UP.
DIDN'T YOU LIKE IT MADE WITH BROTH, THOUGH?
HM...
I JUST FEEL LIKE THE SWEET KIND TODAY.
....
OKAY!
ALL SET HERE TOO!

WHAT DID YOU MAKE?
THAT'S A SECRET.
WELL...
...JUST LOOK FORWARD TO FINDING OUT WHEN YOU OPEN IT AT WORK.
THANKS FOR DOING ALL OF THAT.
NO TROUBLE AT ALL.
THERE WE GO.
...IT'S TIME FOR ME TO LEAVE FOR WORK, THOUGH.
IN THAT CASE...
...WHERE'S MY GOOD-BYE KISS?
YOU REALLY WANT TO BE BABIED TODAY, DON'T YOU?
...DID SOMETHING HAPPEN?

HAVE A GOOD DAY.
YEP! SEE YOU LATER.
ちゅ
CHU (SMOOCH)
DID YOUR DOTING WIFE MAKE YOU ANOTHER SWEET LUNCH TODAY, SENPAI?
WHEN I START EARNING AS MUCH AS YOU DO, I'D LIKE TO KEEP A CUTE GIRL OF MY OWN.
LUCKY!
LUCKY!
IT'S NOT LIKE THAT. THERE'S NOTHING DOTING OR SWEET ABOUT—
GYAH!?
C'MON! IT DOESN'T GET MORE SWEET AND DOTING THAN THAT!
Love
I GUESS SHE DOES DO STUFF LIKE THIS SOMETIMES ...

OH, I'M OFF DURING THIS YEAR'S FIREWORKS SHOW TOO.
WANT TO GO?
BLUEFIN TUNA
....
I MEANT TO THE FIRE-WORKS.
花火大会
FIREWORKS SHOW
THIS SAYS THEY'RE CARVING UP BLUEFIN.
I DON'T THINK WE NEED TO GO, DO WE?
IT'S HOT AND ALL.
IN THAT CASE...
...WANT TO WATCH IT FROM HOME!?
WE CAN SEE IT FROM HERE!?
DIDN'T YOU KNOW?

TA-DAAA!
WHY ARE YOU IN A YUKATA?
I THOUGHT IT WOULD HELP SET THE MOOD.
SINCE WE'RE DOING THIS, WE SHOULD HAVE FUN WITH IT.
OH, HANG ON A SECOND!
夏限定
LIMITED SUMMER RELEASE
ゆるよい
YURUYOI
Suntory
ALCOHOL 3%
WHY NOT HAVE A DRINK...
...WHILE WE WATCH?

A TOAST TO YOUR EYES.
WELL, THEN...
HERE'S TO OUR LOVE, I GUESS.
CHEERS.

IT SURE IS PRETTY.
ISN'T IT?

DID YOU WANT TO GO?
HM?

AND THEY LIVED HAPPILY EVER AFTER!

AFTERWORD

IT'S A PLEASURE TO MEET YOU ALL! I'M KURUKURUHIME!
IT'S HARD TO BELIEVE I'M ACTUALLY WRITING AN AFTERWORD.
PATA (WAVE)
PATA

OH! A FRIEND OF MINE DREW THE LITTLE CRITTER ON MY CREATOR PROFILE FOR ME. SO ADORABLE!
WHEN I STARTED FEELING UNEASY AND ASKED "ARE WE FRIENDS? ARE WE OKAY?", I WAS TOLD, "OF! COURSE! WE! ARE! FRIENDS!" SO WE'RE FRIENDS.

...SO! THIS IS MY FIRST BOOK.

WHILE I WORKED ON THIS BOOK, I DISCUSSED EVERY LITTLE BIT OF IT WITH MY EDITOR, FROM START TO FINISH.
EVERY TIME THIS EDITOR HAS A SUGGESTION, I'M LIKE, "OOH! THAT'S SUCH A TURN-ON!" EVEN WHEN SHE REJECTS AN IDEA, IT DOESN'T MAKE ME SAD. SHE'S TERRIFIC.
CONCEPT DRAWING

WE MOSTLY TALKED VIA E-MAIL, AND THE SUBJECT LINE WAS "YURI COHABITATION PROJECT," WHICH SPURRED ON ALL SORTS OF ODD FANTASIES...
ABOUT THE YURI COHABITATION PROJECT: I'VE MADE A LIST OF CANDIDATE PROPERTIES. WOULD YOU REVIEW THEM?
ALL RIGHT... I'LL DO THAT...
...DUMB, HUH!!?

IN ANY CASE...
THIS BOOK WOULDN'T HAVE MADE IT INTO THE WORLD SAFELY WITHOUT THE HELP OF MANY PEOPLE.
I THINK I'LL SEND THE ENCHANTING EDITORIAL DEPARTMENT SOME CRAB OR SOMETHING ALONG THOSE LINES.
PEKO (BOW)
PEKO

THERE ARE LOTS OF OTHERS I'D LIKE TO THANK TOO...

THE DESIGNER, WHO DESIGNED THIS BOOK BEAUTIFULLY...
EVERYONE WHO WAS INVOLVED IN ITS PRODUCTION...
AND YOU, FOR PICKING IT UP!
SEE YA!
SERIOUSLY, THANK YOU SO MUCH!

Translation Notes

COMMON HONORIFICS

no honorific: Indicates familiarity or closeness; if used without permission or reason, addressing someone in this manner would constitute an insult.

-san: The Japanese equivalent of Mr./Mrs./Miss. If a situation calls for politeness, this is the fail-safe honorific.

-chan: An affectionate honorific indicating familiarity used mostly in reference to girls; also used in reference to cute persons or animals of either gender.

-senpai, Senpai: An honorific used when addressing upperclassmen or more experienced coworkers.

Page 9

Me•Rhythm masks

These are a brand of self-heating, disposable, "steam" eye masks manufactured by Kao.

Page 27

***Mochi* (jealous)**

The visual is a pun; the words for "baked *mochi*" (which is the thing that's sitting on Hotaru's head) and "jealousy" are both pronounced the same way and can be written with the same kanji characters.

Page 37

Lovers' suicide *moe*

Moe is a geeky, fetish-like obsession with something cute, usually a certain category of girl (maids, little sisters) or piece of clothing (glasses, school uniforms). Also used as an interjection when something triggers the obsession.

Page 53

Yandere

This type of person is so romantically obsessed with the object of their affections that their love gives way to violent or murderous tendencies.

Page 54

Akabeko

Traditional toys from Fukushima prefecture that are shaped like red cows.

Page 120

A Couple Even an Ogre Would Smirk Over

"An ogre would smirk over" is a reference to the last half of the phrase, "When you talk about next year, an ogre laughs," meaning "Nobody knows what might happen next year (so there's no point in talking about it)." In this case, the phrase has been modified from "laugh" to "a silly, involuntary grin."

Kurukuruhime

It feels as
if I've gotten help
from all sorts of people,
my readers included, over
the course of this past year.
The people around me are
constantly saving my neck.
Thank you very much.
This is my first book,
and I'd be delighted
if you enjoyed it.

Yuri Life

No Love, No Life!

Kurukuruhime

Translation: Taylor Engel Lettering: Alexis Eckerman

YURIGURASHI
©Kurukuruhime 2018
First published in Japan in 2018 by KADOKAWA CORPORATION, Tokyo.
English translation rights arranged with KADOKAWA CORPORATION, Tokyo through TUTTLE-MORI AGENCY, INC., Tokyo.

Yen Press
150 West 30th Street, 19th Floor
New York, NY 10001

Visit us at yenpress.com
facebook.com/yenpress
twitter.com/yenpress
yenpress.tumblr.com
instagram.com/yenpress

First Yen Press Edition: July 2019

Yen Press is an imprint of Yen Press, LLC.
The Yen Press name and logo are trademarks of Yen Press, LLC.

The publisher is not responsible for websites (or their content) that are not owned by the publisher.

Library of Congress Control Number: 2019938440

ISBNs: 978-1-9753-5727-6 (paperback)
978-1-9753-5729-0 (ebook)

10 9 8 7 6 5 4 3 2 1

LSC-C

Printed in the United States of America